I FOLLOW THE
RULES

BY CHARLOTTE TAYLOR

 Gareth Stevens
PUBLISHING

Please visit our website, www.garethstevens.com. For a free color catalog of all our high-quality books, call toll free 1-800-542-2595 or fax 1-877-542-2596.

Library of Congress Cataloging-in-Publication Data
Names: Taylor, Charlotte, author.
Title: I follow the rules / Charlotte Taylor.
Description: New York : Gareth Stevens Publishing, 2021. | Series: We've
   got character | Includes bibliographical references and index.
Identifiers: LCCN 2019044002 | ISBN 9781538256459 (library binding) | ISBN
   9781538256435 (paperback) | ISBN 9781538256442 (6 Pack) | ISBN 9781538256466
   (ebook)
Subjects: LCSH: Obedience–Juvenile literature.
Classification: LCC BJ1459 .T39 2020 | DDC 179/.9–dc23
LC record available at https://lccn.loc.gov/2019044002

Published in 2021 by
Gareth Stevens Publishing
111 East 14th Street, Suite 349
New York, NY 10003

Copyright © 2021 Gareth Stevens Publishing

Designer: Sarah Liddell
Editor: Megan Quick

Photo credits: Cover, p. 1 GagliardiPhotography/Shutterstock.com; background throughout Igor Vitkovskiy/Shutterstock.com; p. 5 LightField Studios/Shutterstock.com; p. 7 Sergey Novikov/Shutterstock.com; p. 9 Bull's-Eye Arts/Shutterstock.com; p. 11 Yuliya Evstratenko/ Shutterstock.com; p. 13 Syda Productions/Shutterstock.com; p. 15 Pressmaster/ Shutterstock.com; p. 17 George Rudy/Shutterstock.com; p. 19 YAKOBCHUK VIACHESLAV/ Shutterstock.com; p. 21 Monkey Business Images/Shutterstock.com.

All rights reserved. No part of this book may be reproduced in any form without permission in writing from the publisher, except by a reviewer.

Printed in the United States of America

Some of the images in this book illustrate individuals who are models. The depictions do not imply actual situations or events.

CPSIA compliance information: Batch #CS20GS: For further information contact Gareth Stevens, New York, New York at 1-800-542-2595.

Find us on

CONTENTS

Boldface words appear in the glossary.

Why Do We Have Rules?

Lots of places have rules! There are rules at home, at school, and in your neighborhood. We have rules for many reasons. Some rules keep us safe. Other rules help things stay clean and neat. Rules can also give everyone a fair chance.

Safety First

Jake was riding his bike. He came to a busy street. He stopped and got off his bike. He waited for the green light to show that he could cross the street. Jake followed the rules and stayed safe.

Jada was playing in a softball game. It was her turn at bat. Before she got her bat, Jada put on a **helmet**. Each player had to wear a helmet to **protect** their head. Jada followed the rules and did not get hurt.

Isabella's doorbell rang. She looked out the window. She did not know the person at the door. Isabella did not open the door. Her **parents** told her not to open the door to a stranger. Isabella followed the rules and stayed safe.

Let's Be Fair

Luke was playing his **favorite** video game. His mom told him to let his brother play the game after half an hour. Luke wanted to keep playing, but he stopped. Luke followed the rules and gave his brother a chance.

13

Diego's teacher asked the class a question. Diego knew the answer. He did not shout it out. He raised his hand. Diego waited for his teacher to call on him. By following the rules, Diego gave other children a chance to talk.

Take Care

Laila's class took out books from the **library**. The teacher said not to eat or drink near the books. Laila took her book home. She did not read it until after her snack. Laila followed the rules and took care of her book.

David was making a painting. It was time for lunch. The teacher told the **students** to clean up. David put away the paints. He washed the paintbrushes. Then he lined up for lunch. David followed the rules and kept the classroom neat.

Hailey's family had a **picnic** at the park. After they finished eating, they threw away all of the trash from their lunch. Then they played a game of catch. They followed the rules and kept the park clean.

GLOSSARY

favorite: liked best

helmet: a hard hat that keeps your head safe

library: a place where books are kept

parent: a person who is a mother or father

picnic: a meal that is eaten outside

protect: to keep safe

student: a person who goes to a school to learn

FOR MORE INFORMATION

BOOKS

Cook, Julia. *That Rule Doesn't Apply to Me!*. Boys Town, NE: Boys Town Press, 2016.

Smith, Molly. *I Can Follow the Rules.* Pelham, NY: Newmark Learning, 2019.

WEBSITES

Understand the Basic School Rules

video.search.yahoo.com/search/video?fr=yfp-t&p=basic+rules+for+kids#id=1&vid=37c6af130203750a944f4204e882db11&action=click
A fun video shows students going over the rules at school.

Why Do We Have Rules?

www.wonderopolis.org/wonder/why-do-we-have-rules
Take a moment to think about why we have rules and what would happen if we didn't!

Publisher's note to educators and parents: Our editors have carefully reviewed these websites to ensure that they are suitable for students. Many websites change frequently, however, and we cannot guarantee that a site's future contents will continue to meet our high standards of quality and educational value. Be advised that students should be closely supervised whenever they access the Internet.

INDEX